How to Write Term Papers,

For High School and College Students

By Joan Whetzel

Table of Contents

How to Write Term Papers,
for High School and College Students
By Joan Whetzel

Term papers are a mainstay of high school and college education. Teachers assign these papers to help students learn to research and write well, organize their thoughts together clearly, and express ideas in writing. All of these skills are important to have for students just starting many a career after leaving college, especially jobs at the managerial level.

This discussion of term papers is broken down into chapters:

- ***What Are Academic Writing Assignments?*** Helps students understand what the basics of what is expected.
- ***Choosing a Term Paper Topic.*** Discusses assigned topics as well as choosing a topic that is related to the class instructional material.
- ***Researching the Topic.*** Discusses how to perform the research and where to work.
- ***Scholarly Sources.*** Helps students determine whether a resource is considered scholarly.
- ***Tips for Searching the Internet.*** Discusses different ways to search for information on the internet.
- ***Creating a Working Outline.*** Helps students organize the main topics and determine where there is holes in their research.
- ***Organizing the Term Paper.*** Discusses using the outline to organize the term paper and make it more readable.
- ***Writing a Rough Draft.*** The rough draft is the first draft of the paper, which will be edited and refined in later drafts.
- ***The Term Paper Format.*** Using correct format is especially important for college level writing, and in some cases, for professional level writing.

2

- ***Summarizing, Paraphrasing, and Quoting***. Summarizing, paraphrasing, or quoting the works of others is acceptable, but there are rules for doing this correctly.
- ***Parenthetical Citations***. Parenthetical citations allow writers to attribute the summarizations, paraphrasing and quotations to the original writer.
- ***APA, MLA and the Chicago Manual of Style***. These are the main styles of formatting and citation for all academic writing and some professional writing.
- ***Creating a List of Works Cited***. Instructs students on how to create and format a list of all the resources used, which is placed at the end of the term paper.
- ***Appendix - Reliable Website Resources***. These websites are considered to have reliable content, with many of them deemed as scholarly sources.

What Are Academic Writing Assignments?

Understanding the Basics of Academic Writing Assignments

When assigned a writing assignment, it is important for students to understand what is expected of them by the teacher. As soon as the professor hands out the syllabus on the first day of class, begin by scanning through the entire document. Look for the term paper assignment and read through the parameters that the teacher has set up. Understanding the assignment early on, allows students to begin planning their writing assignments as soon as possible so that they can begin working on the term paper a little every day or several days a week. Early planning has an additional benefit, it means that students have the entire semester to get all of their writing assignments done, especially if they have term papers due for more than one class. Lack of planning, on the other hand, could lead to a student having to complete several papers at the end of the semester as well as study for finals. The following steps should help students understand their writing assignments:

1. Read the professor's syllabus instructions one time all the way through.
2. Highlight the main points: the topic (whether assigned by the teacher or chosen by the student); any resources required by the teacher; word count or number of pages; the page format including margins, font type and size; bibliography and citation requirements; and the academic style required by the teacher - APA, MLA, Chicago Manual of Style.
3. Take 1 to 4 lectures to figure out your professor's teaching style., paying attention to phrases he or she uses when emphasizing a point in class. Use these to help guide the researching and writing of the term paper.
4. Pay attention to ideas that the teacher suggests on how to approach the topic.
5. Ask the professor, early on, to clarify whatever is unclear. Most teachers at the college level provide their university e-mail addresses on the syllabus to allow students to ask questions.

6. Examine the instructions for a list of resources required to write the paper, or whether the paper is to be based on required reading for the class.
7. Find out early if the academic paper is be any of the following types of papers: argumentation, straight research, exploratory, annotated bibliography, or book reports, all of which will be different from the essays written for essay exams.

Argumentation

Argumentation papers begin with a thesis (a sentence that states the main idea or argument), the background information to provide context for the argument, supporting evidence for the argument, the counter-arguments or arguments from the opposition, and a section that answers the objections.

Straight Research

These type of papers usually cover topics that are unfamiliar to students. The point these papers is to encourage students become familiar with these new topics, to invite them to learn something new. Students should think of it as an opportunity to conduct a personal investigation and then report back on what they discovered. Think back on the first reading of a book on snakes, dinosaurs, erupting volcanoes, how rainbow's form, and remember how exciting it was to learn about that topic. Take enthusiasm into the research and writing process.

Exploratory

Exploratory papers have one similar aspect to argumentation papers, they both require students to establish an argument and provide supporting evidence. Exploratory papers can also be compared to research papers since both are required to further explore and discuss the argument and its evidence. Exploratory papers begin with a question, followed by background information along with the arguments and supporting evidence that seem to answer the question.

Annotated Bibliography

Annotated bibliographies as an academic paper are rarely assigned, and then, only at the college level. They require students to create a bibliography in MLA, APA or Chicago Manual of Style format as assigned by the professor. But there's one more aspect to this paper; the bibliography must be annotated, meaning the sources are written out in the correct bibliography format and each bibliography entry must include a summary of the argument offered by each source. Annotated Bibliographies, after approval by the teacher, are usually used to write a term paper, thesis or dissertation. They can also be published as is to be used by other students, professors, or researchers to help them discover the best resources for their own academic research.

Book Report

Everyone has been doing these since they attended elementary school. The college level version requires a more extensive exploration of the literature being discussed. It's more or less combination of the book reports most students are familiar with and an exploratory paper. The book report at the college level is a requirement in English and English Lit classes, though some history professors may require something similar for their required reading.

Essays for Exams

Essays for exams require that students have good understanding of the material discussed and read throughout the semester. Attending the lectures, doing the reading, and taking good notes are essential to this type of academic writing. Of course, organizing those notes taken during reading and lectures helps considerably come study time.

Choosing Term Paper Topic

When it comes to writing term papers, one of the most important step is choosing the topic. Some teachers assign topics, which makes starting the paper a little easier. Students can always refine the teacher's topic to fit their own style. In many high school and college classes, though, students are free to choose their own topic. When choosing a topic, weighing the following criteria can help students narrow focus of their topic choice: class subject, the teacher's requirements, the syllabus instructions, the contents of the textbook , and a bit of good old-fashioned brainstorming. The best topics are expansive enough to be interesting and provide ample research materials, yet narrow enough to make the subject more manageable. There's never a wrong topic choice, so long as it it's relevant to the subject being studied and meshes with the teachers' or professor's requirements.

The Class Subject

First off, when deciding a term paper topic, consider the subject of the class for which the paper is being written - literature, English, history, psychology, communications, or social work, for example. This will narrow the topic considerably. Take into account if there is a time frame to the class subject. For instance, American history, which is broken down into two semesters at the college level, begins with the arrival of the colonists to the end of the civil war. The second semester covers the aftermath of the civil war through the present day. The term papers for both of these semesters will clearly cover different, more narrowly defined, topics

The Teacher's Requirements

Most teachers require a minimum page count or word count. They will also require that the paper be typed, single or double spaced, and will expect specific margin widths. Some may have certain resources that must be used as part of the research. Others may have required reading that becomes the basis for topic and primary resource for the term paper.

The Syllabus Instructions

Read through the syllabus instructions to determine the details of the term paper assignment. Teachers usually provide a means for students to ask any questions that come up. The teacher's statement of what will be taught in the class and the list of additional reading materials may suggest a way to choose or refine the topic.

The Textbook Contents

The textbook can serve as a starting point for choosing a topic. Scan the table of contents, chapter headings, and the index in the back of the book for intriguing topic ideas. Try a variation of any of the topics listed or connect one of the topics to another idea, a favorite hobby, or another subject being taken this semester.

Some Old-Fashioned Brainstorming

Discuss topics with other students and observe topic ideas being generated. Exchanging ideas can further refine the topic, whether chosen or assigned

Researching the Term Paper Topic

When writing research papers and term papers, it's good to have a plan of action for the research, note taking and writing process. After all, even professional writers don't just sit down and write the final draft. The writing process starts with the research process. Writers need to locate secondary sources (books, periodicals, internet sources), some primary sources (interviews, surveys, observations, diaries, firsthand accounts of events), collect bibliography information on sources used, and take notes during the research process.

Research Supplies

Besides the resource materials having a few other supplies on hand will help during the research process. A dictionary and thesaurus will help understand the resource materials and a writing style manual will assist the writer in quoting, summarizing and paraphrasing the material as well as creating the bibliography or list of works cited.

Notebooks and pens as well as highlighters are great for taking notes and highlighting important passages on photocopied pages from the resource materials. Index cards are great for organizing bibliography or list of works cited information. (Explanation on how to use the index cards listed below in the bibliography section.)

Having access to a computer, word-processing program and a printer are also important. Some people find it easier to take notes by hand while others find it easier to type in the information. I recommend trying both methods then going with the one that works best for you.

Books

Search the school and public libraries' electronic card catalogs for books that cover the topic chosen for the research or term paper. Check the publication dates on all books. The more recent the publication date, the more accurate the information is deemed to be. You don't want to write a paper based on out of date information.

Checking the card catalogs for books can be done from any computer. It can even be done from home. Create and print out a list of the book titles along with the books' authors and call numbers. Make a note of whether the book is available or checked out. Put in a "hold" request for books that are out or for books that might get checked out before you can get to the library. Also put in inter-library loan requests for books only available at another branch of the public library or at another campus of the school library system. Then when you go to the library the books you need will be ready and waiting for you.

Since reference books cannot be checked out of the library, they require a trip to the library. Look through the materials for the needed information. Obtain a library prepaid card and put some money on it for use at the copy machines. Make copies of the needed pages and be sure to record the bibliography information for each reference book source on the index cards. The benefit of having photocopies is that they can be highlighted and marked on.

Go through the bibliography section at the back of each book. These are the resources used by the books' authors. See which of these books, periodicals and other resources are available at the library, book store or elsewhere. Check into them to see what information can be used to make the research or term paper better.

Periodicals
Periodicals include scholarly journals (i.e. JAMA, Quill), as well as main stream magazines and newspapers. Like books, periodical articles should be fairly recent; written within the last few years ideally. Ask the librarian for help looking up journals and magazines titles, and specific articles for your paper topic. The librarian will be able to tell you if the articles are available in the library or where and how they may be located. Some articles may only be available online or through backordering the issue containing the article. Keep in

mind that ordering back issues and printing articles from the internet costs money.

Internet
Searching the internet for reliable websites and information can be tricky. There is so much information out there and some of the websites are not known for providing reliable or accurate information. Some of the information can be downright misleading or just plain wrong. On top of that, you may discover that many sites copy articles from other sites word-for-word while claiming it's their own work. This is still plagiarism, so don't be tempted to copy their example. The best sites are government websites with a URL ending in ".gov", an academic institution website with a ".edu" URL ending, or any website from a professional organization that deals directly with your topic. A few examples include The Weather Channel, the American Medical Association, the American Heart Association to name a few.

Interviews and Other Primary Research
Primary research involves information the writer personally collects, not re-searched material. Researched material are considered those materials others have already searched for and found. Primary sources include diaries and firsthand accounts of events but they also cover interviews, surveys, observations and analysis performed by the writer of the term paper or research paper.

Interviews are question and answer sessions between the writer and one person or a small group of people (less than 10). *Surveys* are question and answer sessions either performed in person with a large group or, most likely, a written document that the answering people fill out and turn back in to the writer giving the survey. Writers can include their *observations* of events or occurrences, anything that they witnessed themselves firsthand. Observations include descriptions of people, places, events. *Analysis* entails gathering data (mathematical, scientific, social issues), then organizing and examining the information to make sense of it and connect it with the rest of the information used to write the paper.

The Bibliography / List of Works Cited

Once the resources have been chosen,. Make a bibliography entry for each one. Use the index cards for this purpose, one card for each resource. Write out the information for each resource in proper format for a bibliography or list of works cited, depending on the format that the teacher prefers - either APA or MLA.

Separate the cards by resource - books, periodicals, internet, primary resources. Then put them in alphabetical order. Identify each card with a letter and a number. Letter marking: B: books, P: periodicals, I: internet, PS: primary sources. Numbering the cards in the order they appear after they are placed in alphabetical order. So the first book in the index cards would be marked as B1, the 4th periodical in the index cards would be marked P4, the second internet index card gets the marking I2 and the 5th primary resource is called PS5.

Use the card markers to mark identify any quotes, paraphrasing or summarizations you plan to use when writing the paper. This creates a link between the quote, paraphrase or summarized statement and the work being cited. Now that the cards are in order, they can be used to create the list of works cited or bibliography since they were recorded in the correct format.

Scholarly Source

When researching term papers and other academic papers, especially at the college level, teachers usually require students use scholarly sources as part of their research. Scholarly sources are defined as academic works written by educators or anyone studying in a specific area of study. These papers are infused with technical (or field related) jargon. Graphs, charts, and other images are added to expound on the content. Publications containing scholarly sources have no advertising and are not generally intended as reading material for the general public.

Forms of Scholarly Sources

Scholarly sources include professional and academic journals, primary sources (statistical data, lab report), secondary sources (literary reviews; analysis of literary, visual or performing arts scripts and playbills; informed commentary), and tertiary sources (textbooks, encyclopedias, dictionaries). Some sources can be declared scholarly even though they aren't peer reviewed when published by university or academic publishing houses. Scholarly journal articles, unlike popular magazines, include footnotes, endnotes and parenthetical citations.

Sources that Have Been Peer Reviewed

Using peer-reviewed sources offers authority to research papers at the college level by providing the credible information that students can use to back up their arguments. Peer-reviewed sources comprise: essays and articles submitted to journals for publication that have been written by academics, professionals, or experts within the journal's discipline. The articles add to multi-disciplinary discussions by drawing on the results of current research. These scholarly articles must pass through a rigorous peer-review process to determine if the writer's theories and research results meet with the journal's publishing and professional standards.

Using Popular Sources

Popular sources (Popular Photography, Scientific American, Astronomy) are not considered scholarly sources, though they may be deemed as valid resources. Trade magazines geared toward the advertising industry, for example, may include articles relevant to a marketing student's term paper topic. Popular magazines, aimed at mass markets, publish articles on current events and topics of interest to their readers. Since the articles contain current information, they provide excellent current examples to use for further explaining or discussing term paper topics.

Scholarly Sources offer Authority, Structure, Content, Timeliness

Scholarly sources provide *authority*, *structure*, *content*, and *timeliness*. Their *authority* stems from the author's credentials and expertise, the peer-review process, and from the quality of the research done to write the article or book. The scholarly source's writing *structure* also lends credibility to the work through the use of footnotes, endnotes and parenthetical citations show. The scholarly source's *content* includes the information presented in the article, it presents whatever parts of the author's expertise that are relevant to the publication and its readership, and it provides the author's conclusions which have been carefully backed-up documented evidence. *Timeliness* is established through a recent publication date of the scholarly source and by the current makeup of the information provided within the source.

Internet Search Tips

The Associated Press Style Book (2004 edition) description of the internet compares the net to a library containing billions of books which have not been organized in any way, and which doesn't have a card catalog to aid patrons in locating the material they're looking for. This "library" contains an abundance of great information along with a profusion of iffy or downright dreadful information sources. The problem with this set up is that it's difficult to locate the information you need and it can be even more difficult to critically discern which information and which sources are good and which sources are iffy or awful. While exasperating at times, this type of "library search" can also be rewarding due to the amount of information available at your fingertips.

Making Use of Internet Research

The internet provides several methods finding information, including searches through:

- search engines.
- internet directories.
- recognized sites.
- sites of local organizations, educational institutions and companies.
- internet bibliographies and their listed resources.
- posted queries to online groups and social media.

Once the information and the websites have been tracked down, one need only scan through the material in order to evaluate it for accuracy and relevance to the term paper topic. Once it has been determined that the information is valid and valuable, then the website's information can be included in the term paper's bibliography section, which will later be used for citation purposes throughout the paper.

Search Engines

Search engines can be compared to chaotic card catalog where users type in the information they're seeking and let the machine shuffle through the "cards" and dig up the information from the masses of "books" scattered all over the internet. Each search engine has its own databases of websites, which they explore using titles, text, keywords and phrases.

When choosing a search engine, begin with the one with which you are most familiar. Each search engine offers unique ways to locate what you need. So, if the information on one search engine is scarce, then search one or more of the others for further information. By discovering how search engines retrieve the information, they can be used to their utmost potential. The following search engines are some of the most commonly used.

- yahoo.com
- altavista.com
- hotbot.com
- google.com
- askjeeves.com
- dogpile.com

Internet Directories

To further refine internet searches, try using internet directories to locate the key resources relevant to term paper topic. Internet directories contain hierarchical topic menus. Navigate the menus to track down the most suitable resources. The sites chosen for these directories are organized and indexed by humans, making it easier for the search engines to make use of them. The most frequently searched internet directories include:

- INFOMINE
  http://infomine.ucr.edu
- Internet Scout Project
  http://scout.cs.wisc.edu/archives/
- Librarians' Index to the Internet
  http://lii.org/

- looksmart
  http://www.looksmart.com/
- Open Project Directory
  http://dmaz.org/
- WWW.Virtual_Library
  http://vlib.org/
- Yahoo
  http://yahoo.com/

Planning Your Search

Putting together a plan of attack begins with composing the search queries. Brainstorm term paper topic, and completely and concisely define the topic as well. Put together a list of keywords, phrases and questions and begin plugging them into the search line. Consider the following search term styles:

- select specific keywords (nouns)
- choose unusual words relevant to the topic, such as technical terms or names of experts
- type in multiple keywords
- type in a phrase
- ask a question
- incrrectly spell keywords
- use keyword synonyms (crimson instead of red, meteorology instead of weather)
- use the operators *and,* *or* and *not*. Place "and" between two keywords to locate sites include either or both keywords. Use "or" between keywords to find sites with either keyword. Insert "not" between keywords to track down sites containing the first keyword but not the second.

Refine the Search

The initial search for information may not deliver all the necessary information on the term paper's topic. Refine the search terms and give begin again.

1. Narrow the search to more precise features of the topic.

2. Zoom out and search for more general terms related to the topic.
3. Type in wildcards, which includes variations on or root words of the search words (e.g. "heli" for helio, helicopter, helix, helium; "electro" for electronics, Electrolux, electromagnetic, electrolytes, and electrons).
4. Look up the name of the key players related to the topic. Unusual names are more likely to jump to sites with information on the topic.
5. Search for topic related organizations like *NASA* for space, rocket science, solar system, astrophysics, astronomy, and weather topics; the *Weather Channel* or *NOAA* for weather and climate topics; or the *US Geological Survey* for geology, minerals, mining, and earthquake related topics.
6. For unknown web address, make an educated guess by typing in something akin to www.companyname.com (for a company), www.organizationname.org (for an organization), or www.governmentagency.gov (for a government agency), or www.educationalinstitution.edu (for an educational institution.

Avoiding Questionable Resources
The World Wide Web is a massive databank of information in which approximately 25% of the information can be considered reliable, while the other 75% might be deemed questionable at best or complete inaccurate and untrue at worst. As a general rule, it is wise to avoid these questionable sites and pieces of information, however, they may be used *if* there is a specific reason for doing so, or *if* it is disclosed that the information may not be regarded as unreliable. Questionable information can be used as part of an argumentation paper, article, or an op/ed piece discussing both sides of an issue or topic. The questionable info can also be used to discuss for to discuss a topic in depth. For example, if the term paper topic is fantasy and computer games, then including information from a Dungeons and Dragons site may be considered essential.

Determine the reliability of a website's information in the same manner as you would determine the reliability and timeliness of the information in books, magazines and other resources used for research. If it is unclear whether a website, or the information it carries, is reliable, then evaluate the site and the information using the following criteria.

- Locate the page's sponsor and/or author. If neither can be discovered, don't use the site as a resource.
- Look for contact information and follow up on the website's information. If there is no contact information provided, investigate the web site on Whois at www.networgsolutions.com/cgi-bin/whois/whois
- Web addresses ending in ".edu" or ".gov" are generally considered authoritative. If the information provided on a .edu or .gov website does not seem like it belong son an educational or government site, then pass it up and look elsewhere.
- For WebPages that don't openly specify where the information originated from (whether the info is original to the author, organization, or company or if it was "borrowed") then look for the information somewhere else.
- Compare the information to information already known about the topic. If any of the information seems inaccurate, then consider the rest of the information on the site as question able or unreliable.
- If the author demonstrates obvious bias, or if the site includes links to sites demonstrate clear bias, avoid it, unless it's to be used for argumentation or discussion purposes.
- Determine when the webpage was last updated. Websites not updated within the last 5 years are not considered timely. Pages not updated for 10 years or more are considered outdated. The caveat here is that, if updated information is found elsewhere, the older

website's information may be used to illustrate how things have changed over time.

- Establish the website's audience, whether the information provided by the site is written at or near the level that the term paper will be written for. Sites aimed at children contain information is generally too basic and won't supply enough facts or details for a high school or college level paper. Sites aimed at academia, technical audiences, or professional audiences in specialized fields, may be too technical for some students to understand. If it seems too technical, find the information elsewhere, or find someone who can translate the technical jargon.

Creating a Working Outline

The research is done. It's time take the stack of notes and turn it into a great piece of writing, beginning with a first-rate working outline. The main purpose of a working outline is to point out the areas where more research may be needed. The working outline also sets up a roadmap for the term paper layout. If the flow doesn't seem right, it is easier to rearrange or tweak it at the outline stage. The working outline is a form of brainstorming before moving on to the writing stage.

Research, Notes, and Organizing the information.
As you take notes, keep all the bibliography information with the notes for that source. Write the bibliography information in correct bibliography format (the teacher will provide this information with the parameters for the paper; if not ask). After taking copious notes, separate the notes according to the main points. Arrange the notes in order of importance.

Notes can be taken on paper, on index cards, or typed into the computer word processing program. Stack index cards and organize them in the general order that the working outline will take on, placing the main points in separate stacks and holding them together with rubber bands. Cut apart paper notes and organize in the individual note in the same manner as the index cards, sort of like a cut-and-paste outline, and place the main points into separate zipper baggies. With this form of preliminary outlining (the index card and paper note-taking methods) place symbols on each card or slip of paper to indicate which source the info came from, so future reference. This cross-referencing will be needed when it comes time to add parenthetical citations, footnotes and endnotes.

Taking notes on the computer is probably the easiest way to organize them into outline format. First, type the notes into separate files by the bibliography resource entries. Next, copy and paste the notes into the working outline format, as a separate file. As the working outline takes shape, keep asking yourself whether each piece of information fits into the paper's topic and into the teacher's parameters for the term paper. If the piece of information doesn't seem to fit yet, set it aside. When the working outline seems to be complete, take a second look at the pieces of info set aside. If it is obvious that the information doesn't belong, toss it.

Working Outline: The Set Up

Set up the working outline using:

- Roman numerals for the Introduction, the main points and the conclusion
- Capitalized English letters, indented 5 spaces, for the main supporting evidence.
- Arabic numbers, indented by 10 spaces, for details and important information connected to the supporting evidence.
- Lowercase English letters, indented by 15 spaces, for finer points. These points may be included in the final paper if they add to the topic and the flow, or they be deleted if they detract from the term paper.
- Use the main points (the points included with the Roman numerals) as headings in the term paper. This breaks the paper into smaller sections, making it easier to read.

Highlight, use symbols, or write notes in the margin to indicate areas where more research is needed, where some tweaking or re-organization may be needed, or where quotations, end-notes, footnotes, or in-text citations will go. Highlight parts of the working online using different highlighter colors or different text colors, to indicate sections that will be summarized, paraphrased or quoted directly. Make a notation indicating which source the info came from so that it can be cited properly during the writing process. Choose highlighter colors, text colors, and notations that mean something to you, and be consistent.

Read Through the Working Outline

After completing the working outline, set it aside and let rest for a while (1 hour up to several days) depending on the amount of time until the term paper is due. Then return to the outline and read through it, looking for:

- good flow to the material.
- the need for summarization, paraphrasing, and quotes.
- placement of summarizations, paraphrasing, and quotes.
- places where additional research is needed.
- Information that doesn't fit and needs to be deleted.

Some teachers want to see an outline before the actual writing begins. If this is the case, then you have an outline to present. The teacher may identify the good points about the working outline and where work may be needed. Just remember that this is meant as constructive objective criticism which is meant to improve the final draft of the term paper. If the teacher doesn't ask for an outline, then just use it to begin writing the term paper. Remember also that the format of the working outline is not written in stone. It's simply a tool to help organize your research, to reveal potential problems, and show the areas where there may be either too much or too little information. When proceeding to the writing phase, the information in the working outline can always be tweaked until the final paper is the best it can be.

Working Outline Template

I. Introduction
    A. Point #1 summarized
    B. Point #2 summarized
    C. Point #3 summarized

II. Point #1
    A. Supporting Evidence #1
        1. Give details
        2. Give details
        3. Give details

B. Supporting Evidence #2
   1. Give details
   2. Give details
   3. Give details
C. Supporting Evidence #3
   1. Give details
   2. Give details
   3. Give details

III. Point #2
A. Supporting Evidence #1
   1. Give details
   2. Give details
   3. Give details
B. Supporting Evidence #2
   1. Give details
   2. Give details
   3. Give details
C. Supporting Evidence #3
   1. Give details
   2. Give details
   3. Give details

IV. Point #3
A. Supporting Evidence #1
   1. Give details
   2. Give details
   3. Give details
B. Supporting Evidence #2
   1. Give details
   2. Give details
   3. Give details
C. Supporting Evidence #3
   1. Give details
   2. Give details
   3. Give details

V. Conclusion
    A. Point #1 recap
    B. Point #2) recap
    C. Point #3 recap

Organizing the Term Paper

Term paper organization begins with the research and note-taking process. It continues through the stages of creating an outline, writing the rough draft, adding paraphrases, summarizations and quotes, including the citations, editing and proofreading, and creating the bibliography.

Organization Tips for Note Taking

Collect all the research materials together, then begin reading and taking notes. Read through the materials watching for similarities and overlap in content. Take keep note for each resource together with that resource's bibliography information. Make sure you have a dictionary on hand to look up unfamiliar words. Use different colored pens to make notations while hand writing notes, or change text colors when typing in notations on the computer. Highlight key information as necessary. Keep handwritten notes together in a binder or folder. Keep typed in notes together in a folder on your computer's desktop or on a thumb drive. A word of caution, computer's have been known to crash. So keep a copy of your notes on the computer desktop and another copy on a thumb drive as backup.

Outline Organization Tips

Read the previous chapter for complete organization and creation information. In brief, organize the outline around the main arguments or points, followed by supporting evidence, and details. To create an outline, go over the notes and choose three or more main points. As an example, a term paper on refraction might start with a basic outline as follows:

I. Introduction
II. Snell's Law of refraction
III. Rainbows
IV. Prisms
V. Brewster's Optics and Kaleidoscopes
VI. The Visible Spectrum
VII. Conclusion

Fill it in with the supporting evidence in capital letters and details in Arabic numbers. Add notations that cross-reference summarizations, paraphrasing, and quotes to their bibliography card. Then add the notes to fill in the outline. Tweak the outline and reorganize it until the flow looks right. Research any information that seems to be missing, and add it to the outline.

Tips for Organizing the Bibliography Information
As you crack open each new resource, begin by collecting the bibliography information. The exact information you need, and the order that you need to place that information in the bibliography entry, depends on the format that the teacher wants the term paper written in. – American Psychological Association (APA), Modern Language Association (MLA),or the Chicago Manual of Style. If the teacher has no preference, then pick a style for writing the paper and bibliography and stick with it.

Begin by writing the bibliography info at the beginning of the pages of notes. Make a second copy of each bibliography entry on a 3x5 inch index card, in proper format. Make a notation in the upper right-hand corner of the card about the type of resource the entry is (book, periodical, internet website, etc.) so that the entries can be organized by resource type in the final bibliography. Once all the bibliography cards are completely filled out, separate them into individual stacks by resource type. Then place each stack in alphabetical order. Give each card a letter and number notation in the upper left-hand corner that can be used to cross-reference it to any summarizations, paraphrases, or quotations you intend to use. The labeling - system looks something like this:

> B1,B2,B3 etc for books
> P1,P2,P3 etc for periodicals
> I1, I2,I3 etc for internet
> Ps1, Ps2,Ps3 etc for primary sources for periodicals

Either bind the stacks with rubber bands or place them in individual sandwich size zipper baggies. Use the organized stacks to type the bibliography into your computer and save it to the term paper folder.

Writing the Rough Draft

All the research is done, the notes taken, the outline organized, and the bibliography is arranged. Even the decision on quotations, paraphrasing and summarizations have most likely been chosen by this point. It's time to write the term paper's rough draft.

APA, MLA or Chicago Manual of Style?

Check the syllabus or talk to the teacher concerning the preferred writing style for the term paper – APA, MLA, or the Chicago Manual of Style. If the teacher has no preference, then pick one and use it to write the paper and create the bibliography. Either purchase a copy of that stylebook or locate a copy online or at the library. Many college websites include highlights of all three styles. Check out the Purdue University Online Writer's Lab at : http://owl.english.purdue.edu/owl/resource/682/1/

Essentials for Writing the Rough Draft

- Dictionary and Thesaurus
- Preferred Writing Style Manual
- Computer with Word Processing Software
- Printer
- Thumb Drive
- The Working Outline
- The Bibliography
- The Notes

The Introduction

Follow the usual essay format – (1) tell the reader what the term paper is going to talk about, (2) talk about it, and (3) recap what the paper talked about. Use the introduction to introduce the topic of the term paper and the key points, and briefly summarize the sporting evidence. This should all be done in one paragraph containing approximately 4 to 6 sentences.

Section Headings Using the Outline Headings

Section headings are titles used to divide term paper topics into smaller, more manageable bites of information. There should be a minimum of three section headings. Create section heading titles from the outline headings (the headings attached to the Roman numerals). The rough draft section headings don't have to be perfect; they can be perfected during the editing process.

Create Paragraphs from the Outline

Use your outline to write the rough draft paragraphs. Each of the Capitol letters should make 1 to 3 paragraphs. Each paragraph begins with a topic sentence, backed up with the supporting evidence, and filled in with the details and examples. Don't try to get it down perfectly. Just get the ideas down on the page and save the perfecting for the editing and final draft.

Add Quotes, Paraphrasing, and Summarization

Add the summarizations, paraphrasing, and quotes in the appropriate points. Interlace them into the text as a way of using other writers' words help you tell the story. Give the authors their attribution by citing the bibliographical reference as a parenthetical citation, footnotes, or endnotes as appropriate for the style book you are using.

Write the Conclusion

Attach a concluding paragraph to the end of the rough draft that recaps the introduction and the discussion of the topic in the term paper. Write your conclusion at the end of the paper. Close the final paragraph and the term paper with one final, fundamental point. Make it thought provoking.

Give the Term Paper a Working Title

Like the section headings, the working title should reflect the content of the term paper as a whole. It doesn't have to be perfect, the perfect title will make itself know as the editing and proofreading process continues. The working title, like the rough draft, is a work in progress.

Set the rough draft aside and let it rest. This length of the rest period will depend on how much time you have left for editing and writing the final draft. Starting the term paper early provides extra time to finish the term paper, including rest periods, editing and fine tuning.

Summarizing, Paraphrasing, and Quoting

When writing term papers, especially at the college level, teachers may require summarization, paraphrasing and direct quotations from the resources used to write the paper. Summarizing, paraphrasing, and quoting are three ways to use another writer's words and ideas legally, so long as the summarized, paraphrased or quoted passages are attributed to that writer. That means the passages must be cited in a parenthetical citation, a footnote, or an endnote, which is cross-referenced to the bibliography at the end of the term paper.

Summarizing

To summarize another author's work, write a brief version of that author's words and ideas in a manner that is similar to the way the author stated it. This shows that the writer of the term paper understands an is able to explain what the summarized author was trying to say. The basic format for summarizing an author's words is to state the author's last name, the title of the resource (book, periodical article, internet article), then give the brief interpretation of the author's words (in about 1 to2 sentences).

Paraphrasing

To paraphrase anther author's work, make use of a passage that ranges anywhere from one sentence to a paragraph in length. Take the author's words and restate them in your own words. Attribute the paraphrased passage by: (1) providing the author's last name as part of the paraphrasing and include the page number(s) where the passage may be located in the resource, placed in parenthesis at the end of the sentence; or (2) providing the author's last name, author's first name and page numbers in parenthesis at the end of the sentence, before the period.

Quoting

To directly quote another author's work that is about 1 to 2 sentences in length, place quotation marks before and after the quoted passage, along with the author's name (According to Soandso, "quote."). To directly quote either a partial or full paragraph, set the passage apart from the term paper text by indenting both the left and right sides of the paragraph by 5 to 10 spaces. Separate the indented paragraph from the term paper text by one space above and below the quoted passage. Cite the quoted paragraphs by providing the author's last name, author's first name, and page number, in parenthesis, at the end of the last sentence, before the period.

Citation Basics

College professors usually insist on one of three formats for writing and citing term papers - APA, MLA and Chicago Manual of Style. If you don't have your own copy of any of these books, there are four choices: (1) buy a copy of the style book, (2) borrow one from someone else, (3) go the library reference section and use theirs, in the library of course, or (4) go online and try to locate a full copy online or a website (like the Purdue Online Writing Lab) that provides the basics of the writing and citation formats.

MLA Format

Begin paraphrasing and summarizations with a phrase like "John Doe says..." or "According to the John Doe Society..." Surround short quotes (1 to 2 sentences) with quotation marks. Indent longer quotations (a paragraph or longer) on both the left and right sides by to 10 spaces and separate the long quote from the term paper text above it and below it.

Citations for paraphrased, summarized, and quote material belong at the end of the last sentence and before the period. Enclose citations inside parenthesis. The basic format is shown below. However, for more specific citation formats (multiple works by the same author, multivolume works, the Bible or other Holy Book, non-print sources, different authors with the same last name), always consult the MLA style book.

Basic MLA citation format:

- **Single Author**: (author last name, page number)
- **Multiple Authors** (Author #1 last name, Author #2, Author #3, page number)
- **Organization** (Organization name, page number if available - websites are frequently not paginated)
- **No author** (title shortened and italicized, page number)

APA Format

Paraphrasing, summarizing and directly quoting source material is done in much the same way as with MLA format, using parenthetical citations placed at the end of the sentence or paragraph. In general, use a single author's name, multiple author's names, an organization's name, and titles within parenthesis along with the year of publication and a page number, if available, within parenthesis at the end of the last sentence, but before the period.

Basic APA citation format:

- ***Singe Author***: (Simon, 1945).
- ***Multiple Authors***: (Simon & Schuster, 1955).
- ***No Author***: ("The World Almanac", 2011).
- ***Citing a Precise Page*** : ("The Merk Manual", 2010, p. 535).

Chicago Manual of Style Format

The Chicago Manual of Style replaces uses footnotes or endnotes, rather than parenthetical citations. Footnotes appear at the bottom of the same page as the cited material. Endnotes appear on a separate page at the end of the term paper, but before the bibliography page. Unless the professor states a preference, choose whichever method i easiest for you - the footnotes or endnotes. Each footnote or endnote is delegated a superscript notation number, which is positioned at the end of the cited passage. Word processing programs, like Word for Windows, automatically number each citation in succession, and matches them up with the numbered footnote or endnote. If a citation is moved to another location within the term paper, all citations (along with their endnote or footnote) are automatically renumbered in correct numerical order.
 system to place the superscript notations and the footnotes and endnotes in numerical order.

Chicago Manual of Style format has different formats for (a) the firs citation for a source, (b) a source's second citation posted later in the paper, and (c) consecutive citations by the same author as listed below. The numbers at the end of each citation are the page where the passage can be found. (The term Ibid. is Latin, meaning "in the same place.")

Basic Chicago Manual of Style Format:
- **First Citation:**
  [1] Trotter, David. The Screenwrite's Bible. 125-29.
- **Second Citation later in the paper:**
  [5] Trotter. Screenwriter's Bible. 203.
- **Consecutive Citations:**
  [1] Trotter, David. The Screenwriter's Bible. 125-29.
  [2] Ibid. 45.
  [3] Ibid. 110.

It is important to note that all citations (parenthetical citations, footnotes, endnotes) need to correspond to a full Bibliography or List of Works Cited entry. It is also crucial to be aware that, under certain circumstances, citations are not require because they are used so often or are so familiar to the intended reader(s). These conditions include:
- common proverbs - "like a pearl before swine")
- commonly used quotations - "Give me liberty or give me death!"
- facts that are common knowledge - "The Bill of Rights contain the first 10 amendments to the US Constitution"

The Basic Term Paper Format

First and foremost, when writing a term paper, always follow the teacher's preferred formatting, whether it be APA, MLA, or Chicago Manual of Style. Then follow that style book's directions for setting up the paper, adding citations, and creating a Bibliography or List of Works Cited. Generally speaking, in academic settings:

- the APA format is used to write papers in the social sciences: psychology, sociology, anthropology, or business.
- the MLA format is applied to the papers written for classes in the humanities: English, history, literature, philosophy, religion, and the visual and performing arts).

Materials & Typeface

Type all term papers on plain white paper measuring 8.5 x 11 inches Use Times New Roman type face and 12-point font, unless the teacher states otherwise, and boldface for titles and section headings Double space and create 1 inch margins to the left and right of the text as well as at the top and bottom of the page. Follow the teacher's instructions for adding page numbers. Ask the teacher whether he or she prefers the term paper to be bound with a paper clip, staples, a binder or a brad-style folder.

Title Page and Identification

The teacher will specify whether a title page is required or whether he or she prefers the student's name, class ID number, and title (or other information) should go on the first page.

MLA Format requires no title page Instead follow this format:
  Title (*flush left*) **and Page number** (*flush right*)
  Author's Name
  Instructor's Name
  Course Name and Number

APA format requires a title page begins with a shorter version of the title. Page numbers are placed at the top of the page, flush right, beginning with Page 1 on the title page. The rest of the information is double-spaced and centered on the page as follows:

Full Title
Author's Name
Class and Course Number
Institutional Affiliation
Instructor's Name
Date

Punctuation & Typing

For both APA and MLA, allow for one space after words, commas, colons, semicolons, periods, question marks and between dots in ellipses (... *space*). Create a dash by typing two hyphens with a space before the first dash and a space after the second dash. When hyphenating two words together (i.e. double-spaced) do not put spaces before or after the hyphen.

Abstracts (APA only)

An abstract page is required only for papers written in APA, and only if the teacher requests one. Begin the abstract page with a page header (shortened title and a page number, the word "Abstract" double-spaced and centered after the header, followed by another double spacing and summarization of the term paper approximately 75 to 100 words in length. The summary should include the term paper's main idea, the key points that will be discussed, and it should provide hints about what the research means or the research's applications.

Headings

Break the material into smaller sections and give each section its own title (called a header) which relates the information in that section back to the introductory paragraph and the main title. Like the main title, only the main words in the headings are capitalized.

Visuals

Visuals are defined as anything that helps explain the material but is not part of the text. Visuals include: tables, figures, graphs, charts, maps, drawings and photos. Visuals set this data apart from the main text, making the term paper easier to read while still including the relevant explanatory data and pictures.

Order of Pages and Documentation

Before turning in the term paper, make certain the pages are placed in the correct order as follows:

1. Title Page
2. Abstract (APA only)
3. First Page of the Text
4. Endnotes (Chicago Manual of Style only)
5. References (Bibliography, List of Works Cited)
6. Tables
7. Figures
8. Appendices

Writing the Final Draft of the Research Paper

The research is done, the working outline completed, the term paper rough draft has been written. It's time to edit, proofread, spell and grammar check that rough draft and make it a polished final draft.

Items to Have on Hand
Bring these items to the table to help the refining process go more smoothly:
- a dictionary for double-checking and correcting spelling and word usage
- a thesaurus to steep the writing with richer verbs and nouns
- the writings style manual (APA, MLA, Chicago Manual of Style) to correct any style or format errors in the term paper
- a computer with word processing software to make the writing process more quickly and easily
- a printer for producing a hard copy of the final term paper to hand into the teacher
- a thumb drive to save the final draft

The General Approach
1. First, set the rough draft aside and take a break, anywhere from 15 minutes to a couple o days.
2. Next. spend a the time getting a snack or a drink. stretching your legs, taking a nap or getting a good night's sleep - whatever it takes to clear your head and return to the term paper with fresh eyes and a refreshed brain. Remember to save enough time to complete the corrections and go over the final draft without speeding through the process.
3. Silently read through the term paper, correcting any glaring errors in spelling, grammar, sentence flow, or paragraph flow.
4. Read the term paper out loud, which enables your ear to hear what it sounds like. Listen for any mistakes that your eyes might have missed.

5. Have a friend or family member read through the paper. This provides another perspective and a fresh set of eyes to spot any problems that may have been missed.

6. Now that you know what needs tweaking, edit the term paper for any remaining mistakes, further proofread it for any additional smaller errors, and tweak it again tweak for flow to produce final term paper that makes sense.

Refine the Introduction and Conclusion

Begin with the introduction. Rectify spelling, grammar and sentence structure problems and adjust the wording to make the term paper's opening paragraph exciting, and make the reader and want to keep reading. Use the thesaurus to help come up with the creative word choices. Do the same for the conclusion, bringing the paper to a equally vivacious close.

Editing Ideas, Organizing, and Writing to Style

Check each paragraph's topic sentence to make sure the paragraph points are sufficiently introduced. Read the paragraph's through for flow and to make sure the rest of each paragraph supports its topic sentence. Correct any obvious topic sentence, supporting evidence, and flow errors.

Edit for Grammar and Spelling Errors

After the initial editing for major errors, use your computer's word processor to run a grammar and spell check. This will clear up most of the spelling and grammar problems. Read the paper again with an eye for spotting additional - smaller - grammar and spelling problems that may have been missed. Check for mistakes like:

- missing words
- double words (places a word may have been written the word twice in a row)
- run on sentences
- sentence fragments
- unnecessary or misused comma or semi-colon splices
- subject / verb agreement
- pronoun / reference agreement

- correct use of apostrophes (for contractions, plurals, and words showing possession)
- words with reversed "ei / ie"
- homonyms (words that sound alike but are spelled differently) such as: they're / their / there; write / rite / right; here / hear; steal / steel; affect / effect; allusion / illusion; capitol / capital; cereal / serial; click / clique; climactic / climatic; defuse / diffuse; eminent / imminent; faze / phase; flair / flare; flew / flu / flue; formally / formerly; forth / fourth; hardy / hearty; ingenious / ingenuous; lead / led; liable / libel; loose / lose; miner / minor; peak / peek / pique; plain / plane; principle / principal; role / roll; troop / troupe; veil / vale; who's / whose.

Cross-Reference Quotations, Paraphrasing and Summarizations with the Bibliography

Check all quotes, paraphrasing and summarizations, and the citations created during the rough draft writing, be sure they are properly cited. Parenthetical citations, footnotes, and endnotes should be properly formatted according to the style book used to write the term paper.

Double-Check the Bibliography / List of Works Cited

Read through the entries in the Bibliography or List of Works Cited. They should be written in proper format, grouped according to resource type (book, periodical, letters, interviews, internet sources, other electronic sources, etc.) under the grouping's heading, and each grouping should be placed in alphabetical order.

Let the term paper rest again -for a few minutes - then return to read through the entire final draft of the term paper, tweaking it if necessary. If you need help with writing, style or editing problems, remember that most universities have great writing lab resources available through the library. Check out the resources offered by the Purdue University Online Writing Lab at:
http://owl.english.purdue.edu/owl/resource/682/1/

Creating the List of Works Cited

All term papers must include reference list, also known as a Bibliography or a List of Works Cited. This list is placed at the end of the paper, separated from the text and started on a new page, and titled "References," "Bibliography," or "List of Works Cited," centered at the top of the page. The title should be capitalized but should not include boldface, underlining, quotation marks, or italics. Every source used to write the term paper needs a bibliography entry.

The basic format is to double-space between entries, placing the first line of each entry flush left, and then indenting succeeding lines 1/2 inch or 5 spaces. Separate the entries by categories and then alphabetize all entries under each category. Bibliography entries have different formats that are specific to the category (books, periodicals, encyclopedias, internet, etc.). Refer to the APA, MLA, and Chicago Manual of Style books for each category's format. Be aware that the format for electronic sources (internet, e-mails, computer software, online forums, blogs) and electronic media (MP3, Kindle, CDs, DVD Movies, PDFS, JPEGS) vary from print media in that a URL must be included as part of the entry, as well as the date that the book, article, or other electronic resource was accessed. The online version is show below. If the resource is a print version, then the URL and Date Accessed are *not* included in the entry.

APA Bibliography Format

Articles from Periodicals
Author, A. & Author, B. (Publication Date). Article Title. *Online Periodical Title, volume   number* (issue number if one exists). URL Date accessed.

Bernstein, M. (2002). 10 Tips on writing the living Web. *A list apart: For people who make websites, 149.* http://www.alistapart.com/articles/writeliving. Accessed 6/2/2012.

Newspaper Article
Author, A. (Year, Month Day). Article Title. *Newspaper Title.* URL
Date Accessed

Radcliffe, Jennifer. (2011, August21). Lessons for parents for the
new school year. *Houston Chronicle.*
http://www.chron.com/news/houston-texas/article/Lessons-for-
parents-for-new-school-year-2134435.php Date Accessed
6/2/2012.

Books
Author, First Name. *Title.* (Format, if other than print). Publishing
location: Publishing House, Publication Date. Page number.
[This is the print version]

Author, First Name *Title.* URL Date Accessed.

Stockett, Kathryn. *The Help.* (Kindle Format).
Ahttp://www.amazon.com/The-Help-
ebook/dp/B002YKOXB6/ref=sr_1_1?s=digital-
text&ie=UTF8&qid=1313938371&sr=1-   1#_
Date Accessed: 6/2/2012.

Encyclopedias and Dictionaries
Bibliography. *Merriam Webster Dictionary.* 2011 Edition.
http://www.merriam-
webster.com/dictionary/bibliography?show=0&t=1313951382
Date Accessed 6/2/2012.

Computer Software for Specialized Software
Purchased package:
Ludwig, T. (2002). Psych Inquiry [computer software]. New York:
Worth.

44

Downloaded package:
Hayes, B., Tesar, B., & Zuraw, K. (2003). OTSoft: Optimality
Theory Software (Version 2.1)   [Software]. Available from
http://www.linguistics.ucla.edu/people/hayes/otsoft/

E-Mail
APA does not include E-Mail entries in the bibliography. These are
cited only in the body of the paper.

Online Discussion Board (forum)
Frook, B.D. (1999, July 23). New inventions in the cyberworld of
toylandia [Msg 25].
        Message posted to
http://groups.earthlink.com/forum/messages/00025.html

Blog Posting
TenBrook, Catherine. Humor Me [Blog]. Downloaded from:
http://www.myspace.com/quackalishus/blog

Movie
Producer, P. P. (Producer), & Director, D. D. (Director). (Date of
    publication). *Title of motion picture* [Motion picture]. Country of
    origin: Studio or distributor.

Scorseese, M. (Producer), & Lonegran, K. (Writer/Director). (2000).
You can count on   *me* (Motion Picture) [DVD].
United States: Paramount Pictures.

Recorded Music
Songwriter, W. W. (Date of copyright). Title of song [Recorded by
artist if different from song   writer]. On *Title of album* [Medium of
recording]. Location: Label. (Recording date if   different from
copyright date).

Shocked, M. (1992).Over the Waterfall, on *Arkansas Traveler*. [CD]
New York: PolyGram Music.

45

Maroon 5. Moves Like Jagger Hands, on *Hands All Over*. [MP3}.
ASIN: B0059H09DC

MLA Bibliography Format, Electronic Resources
Important Note: Online resources no longer require URLs in MLA
format. This is because websites change frequently. Entries need to
include basic information author(s), article name, website name,
version number, publisher information, page number (if listed),
medium of publication (DVD, CD, Web, etc.) and download date.
Some professors may still require URLs, in which case enclose the
URL in <angle brackets>.

Books
Aristotle. *Poetics*. Trans. S. H. Butcher. *The Internet Classics
Archive*. Web Atomic and   Massachusetts Institute of Technology,
13 Sept. 2007. Web. 4 Nov. 2008.   ⟨http://classics.mit.edu/⟩.

For print books include the Location of Publication: Publishing
House, Copyright Date. Page Number(s). after the title.

E-Mail
TenBrook, Catherine. "Re: Architectural Drawings." Message to the
author. 29 Aug., 2011. E-   mail.

Discussion Groups (forums)
Editor, screen name, author/ compiler (if listed). "Title of posting."
Forum Site Name. Version   number (if listed). Institution/
Organization associated with the site. Medium of   publication.
Download date.

Digital files (PDF, MP3, JPEG)
Smith, George. "Pax Americana: Strife in a Time of Peace." 2005.
Microsoft Word file.

Bentley, Phyllis. "Yorkshire and the Novelist." *The Kenyon Review* 30.4 (1968): 509-22.
     JSTOR. PDF file.

Maroon 5. Moves Like Jagger Hands, on *Hands All Over*. [MP3}.
ASIN: B0059H09DC
     Downloaded from Amazon http://www.amazon.com/Moves-Like-
     Jagger/dp/B0059H09DC/ref=sr_1_5?ie=UTF8&s=dmusic&q id=1313952847&sr=1-5

Recorded Sound
Shocked, M. Over the Waterfall, on *Arkansas Traveler*. New York: PolyGram Music (1992).   CD.

Movie
Title. Director. Actors. Distributor. Year of Release. Medium.

Chicago Manual of Style, Electronic Resources
Internet Article and Website
Radcliffe, Jennifer.. "Lessons for parents for the new school year." Houston Chronicle. <http://www.chron.com/news/houston-texas/article/Lessons-for-parents-for-new-school-year-2134435.php> (21 August 2011).

"Google Privacy Policy," last modified March 11, 2009, http://www.google.com/intl/en/privacypolicy.html.

For print versions, include the Date, Page number, Volume Number after the name of the publication (e.g. Houston Chronicle).

E-Mail
TenBrook, Catherine. <cattenbr@yahoo.com> "Architectural Drawings." Personal E-mail.
     29 Aug., 2011.

Listserv and Newsgroup
Wirth, Ann Welpton. < afwirth@sunset.backbone.olemiss. edu >
"Desserts." 27 May 1997. < asle@unr.edu > (28 May 1997).

< kunk@astro.phys. unm.edu > "What Did the Vandals Learn?" 30
May 1997.   <soc.history.ancient> (2 June 1997).

FTP Files
Wang, Zheng. "EIP: The Extended Internet Protocol: A Long-
Term Solution to Internet   Address Exhaustion." June 1992. <
ftp://munnari.OZ.AU/big- internet/eip.txt >
        (5 June 1997).

Movie
Scorseese, M. (Producer), & Lonegran, K. (Writer/Director). (2000).
You can count on   me (Motion Picture) [DVD].
United States: Paramount Pictures.   '

Recorded Music
Shocked, M. (1992).Over the Waterfall, on *Arkansas Traveler*. [CD].
New York: PolyGram Music.

As you can see, the formula for electronic format resources varies
from one stylebook to the next, which illustrates the necessity of
double checking the stylebook frequently as you progress through
the writing process. Some professors deduct points for even the
smallest transgressions in spelling, grammar, paper format, and in
citation and bibliography format. Yes, the term paper can be
organized after it is written, but it is easier to learn the basics ahead
of time, and then make a regular habit of writing, organizing and
citing in the proper format as you go. For additional help creating
bibliographies, try one of these websites:
   • Microsoft Office 2007 Help and How-to, "Create a
        Bibliography"
   http://office.microsoft.com/en-us/word-help/create-a-
        bibliography-HA010067492.aspx

- Purdue: OWL, "Annotated Bibliographies
  http://owl.english.purdue.edu/owl/resource/614/01/

Appendix – Trustworthy Website Resources

While doing my own researching and writing over the years, both in college and in professional writing, I have found several helpful websites that are trustworthy and that can be considered reputable resources. These sites, which fall into several categories, can used by writers, students, and educators alike.

Writing Websites
Purdue University Online Writing Lab (OWL)
http://owl.english.purdue.edu/owl/
Contains a collection of resources for researchers, writers, and instructors. Though primarily created for Purdue University students and faculty, it allows free worldwide access, and it's easy to navigate.

Merriam Webster Dictionary
http://www.merriam-webster.com/
The online reads much like the print version, however, instead wading through a entire page's entries, single words or phrases can be located by typing them into the site's search box. The site includes a thesaurus, encyclopedia, a medical dictionary, a Spanish-English dictionary, a word game tab, a slang term dictionary, and a new word dictionary.

Roget's Thesaurus
http://thesaurus.com/Roget-Alpha-Index.html
Not quite as comprehensive as the print version, the online version is still helpful in locating synonyms and antonyms for commonly used words and phrases

The U.S. Copyright Office
http://www.copyright.gov/
This site contains all aspects of copyrights, copyright law, copyright records, licensing, registration, as well as filing for copyrights, patents, trademarks, royalties and anything else related to copyrights and intellectual property protection.

The Chicago Manual of Style
http://chicagomanualofstyle.org/CMS_FAQ/new/new_questions01.html
The online version of the style manual, available by yearly subscription.

American Psychological Association (APA) Style Manual
http://apastyle.org/
The online version of the APA Style Manual. Contains the basics, but not the full detailed information available in print.

Modern Language Association (MLA) Style Book
http://www.mla.org/
The online version of the MLA Style Book. Requires an activation code to access the site.

Associated Press (AP) Style Book
http://www.ap.org/
The online version of the style book for journalists.

Society for Professional Journalism (SPJ)
http://spj.org/
Contains resources, training, and legal issues for journalists.

Library and General Reference Websites
American Fact Finder
http://factfinder2.census.gov/faces/nav/jsf/pages/index.xhtml
Contains U.S. demographic information.

Library Thing
http://www.librarything.com/
Great for book lovers to upload a catalog of all the books on their shelves, get involved in book discussions, or find suggestions for new reading material.

Ref Desk
http://www.refdesk.com/index.html
Referred to as the "fact checker for the internet." Has links to search engines and websites for double checking your facts, or finding difficult to locate facts.

Library of Congress
http://www.loc.gov/library/libarch-digital.html
Includes access to print, pictorial, and audio-visual collections, as well as other digital services and library resources in digital format.

Math and Science Websites

NASA
http://www.nasa.gov/
Everything space related: space flight, the International Space Station, the Jet Propulsion Lab, the Johnson and Kennedy Space Centers, astronauts and astronaut training, astronomy, comparative planetology, the Hubble Space Telescope, satellites, space phenomena (solar flares, auroras(, and even weather, which affects take offs and landings as well as communications with satellites, space vehicles and the ISS.

National Oceanic and Atmospheric Administration (NOAA)
http://www.noaa.gov/
Covers anything weather and geology.

United States Geological Survey (USGS)
http://www.usgs.gov/
Covers geology and geography.

The Weather Channel
http://www.weather.com/
Contains a number of great weather resources: facts and figures, documentaries, written material.

National Geographic Maps
http://maps.nationalgeographic.com/maps
The organization that prints the magazine and all those great maps. All the magazines, articles and maps are available online. Also provides some terrific digital maps that are even better than the print version.

Geography, Social Studies and History Websites
Internet4Classrooms - Geography Websites
http://www.internet4classrooms.com/social_geography.htm
Provides links to maps, landforms, countries and continents.

Central Intelligence Agency (CIA) World Fact Book
https://www.cia.gov/library/publications/the-world-factbook/
An almanac of sorts, the CIA World Fact Book supplies this information on over 267 countries: history, people,

government, economy, geography, communications, transportation, military, and trans-national issues.

History, Arts and Culture
http://www.usa.gov/Citizen/Topics/History.shtml
Learn about art, architecture, culture, ethnic groups, history, libraries, and museums in the US.

History World - Histories and Timelines
http://www.historyworld.net/
Look up historical information and timelines.

USA.gov - The Official Website of the U.S. Government
http://www.usa.gov/
Has links to the various government agencies and information on the US government by topic.

Commerce and Trade
US Department of Commerce
http://www.commerce.gov/
Has links to information on U.S. trade, commerce and the economy.

International Trade Administration
http://trade.gov/
Covers international trade, commerce and the economy.

World Trade Organization (WTO)
http://www.wto.org/
The WTO regulates international trade and commerce and this site include the rules governing world trade and how the WTO works

International Organizations
North Atlantic Treaty Organization (NATO)
http://www.nato.int/cps/en/natolive/index.htm
NATO governs the world's politics and military alliances. A great resource for information in international politics.

United Nations (UN)
http://www.un.org/en/

The UN is an organization that fights for human rights. The site covers humanitarian issues and human rights issues.

Policing and Security Agencies

Interpol
http://www.interpol.int/
Interpol is the international policing agency responsible for investigates crime on an international level.

CIA
https://www.cia.gov/
The CIA site conducts international investigates, intelligence, and security for the US.

FBI
http://www.fbi.gov/
The FBI operates on an national level, investigating crimes and gathering intelligence within US borders.

Department of Homeland Security
http://www.dhs.gov/index.shtm
Homeland Security is responsible for keeping the US and its borders safe.

Wikileaks
http://wikileaks.org/
One could argue, perhaps, that Wikileaks acts sort of like a media version of a policing agency for trying to keep government in check and keeping freedom of the press alive - even if that means coming dangerously close to crossing a fine line on reporting things that the government doesn't want published. On the other hand, some of the stories produced on Wikileaks could potentially produce security risks or provide information to enemies of the US. With this in mind, use this site and its information with caution.

Bibliography

Books
Gibaldi, Joseph. *MLA Handbook for Writers of Research Papers. Fifth Edition.* New York: Modern Language Association of America, 1999.

Goldstein, Norm, Editor. *The Associated Press Stylebook.* New York: Basic Books, 2004.

Hacker, Diana. *A Writer's Reference, Third Edition.* Boston: Bedford Books, 1995.

Publication Manual of the American Psychological Association. Fifth Edition. Washington DC: American Psychological Association 2001.

Internet
Burgett, Bruce. University of Washington Bothell: *Critical Reading Strategies for Scholarly Sources.* Accessed: 6/23/2012. http://library.uwb.edu/guides/criticalreadingscholarly.html

Capitol Community College. *A Guide for Writing Research Papers Based on Modern Language Association (MLA) Documentation.* Accessed: 6/23/2012. http://www.ccc.commnet.edu/mla/index.shtml

Cornell University Library. *APA Citation Style.* Accessed: 6/23/2012. http://www.library.cornell.edu/resrch/citmanage/apa

Custom Writings. *How to Write and Exploratory Essay.* Accessed: 6/23/2012. http://www.customwritings.com/blog/types-of-essays/write-exploratory-essay.html

Duke University Libraries. *Citing Sources.* Accessed: 6/23/2012.
http://library.duke.edu/research/citing/within/apa.html

Eastern Kentucky University. *The Argumentative Paper.*
http://people.eku.edu/williamsf/RhetSum/default.htm   Accessed:
6/23/2012.

Edu Choices. *25 Websites for Student Researchers and News
Hounds.* Accessed: 6/23/2012.
http://educhoices.org/articles/25_Websites_for_Student_Researchers
_and_News_Hounds.html

Edu Choices. *50 of the Best Websites for Writers.* Accessed:
6/23/2012.
http://educhoices.org/articles/50_of_the_Best_Websites_for_Writers
.html

Education Insider. *25 Legitimately Useful Sites for College Students.*
Accessed: 6/23/2012.
http://education-
portal.com/articles/25_Legitimately_Useful_Sites_for_College_Stud
ents.html

Essay Paper. *Definition Essay.* Accessed: 6/23/2012.
http://www.essay-paper.net/definition_essay.html

Essay Town. *Citation of Research Paper.* Accessed: 6/23/2012.
http://www.essaytown.com/writing/citation-of-research-paper

Franklin Pierce. *Scholarly Sources.* Accessed: 6/23/2012.
http://library.franklinpierce.edu/research/scholarly.html

Klems, Brian A. *Writer's Digest Online.* "101 Best Websites for
Writers." Accessed: 6/23/2012.
http://www.writersdigest.com/wp-
content/uploads/2011/06/101BestWebsites101.pdf

Media Awareness Network. *How to Search the Internet Effectively.* Accessed: 6/23/2012.
http://bsesrv214.bse.vt.edu/Grisso/Ethiopia/Lectures/Internet/Search_Internet_1.pdf

Purdue University: Purdue Online Writing Lab. *Chicago Manual of Style, 16th Edition.* Accessed: 6/23/2012.
http://owl.english.purdue.edu/owl/resource/717/01/

Purdue Online Writing Lab. *Common Writing Assignments.*
http://owl.english.purdue.edu/owl/section/1/3/ Accessed: 6/23/2012.

Russell, Tony, Allen Brizee, and Elizabeth Angeli. Purdue University Writing Lab. *MLA Formatting and Style Guide.* Accessed: 6/23/2012.
http://owl.english.purdue.edu/owl/resource/560/1/

Purdue University. *Purdue Online Writing Lab.* Accessed: 6/23/2012.
http://owl.english.purdue.edu/owl/search.php

St. Vincent's College: *What Makes an Information Source Scholarly?* Accessed: 6/23/2012.
http://www.stvincentscollege.edu/aboutsvc/infosourcescholarly.cfm

Sylvan Learning Centers. *Top 10 Math Websites.* Accessed: 6/23/2012.
http://tutoring.sylvanlearning.com/newsletter/0704/math.cfm

University of Illinois, Urbana-Champaign: *Is It Scholarly?* Accessed 6/23/2012.
http://www.library.illinois.edu/ugl/howdoi/scholarly.html

University of Toronto. *Research Using the Internet.* Accessed: 6/23/2012.
http://www.writing.utoronto.ca/advice/reading-and-researching/research-using-internet

Made in the USA
Lexington, KY
09 June 2018